Cadaver Dogs

Also by Rebecca Loudon:

Tarantella (Ravenna Press)

Radish King (Ravenna Press)

Navigate, Amelia Earhart's Letters Home (No Tell Books)

Cadaver Dogs

Rebecca Loudon

No Tell Books
Reston, VA

Copyright © 2008 by Rebecca Loudon

Published by No Tell Books, LLC

notellbooks.org

All rights reserved

ISBN: 978-0-615-24969-8

Cover Design: Maureen Thorson

Cover Art: Scott Odom

Proofreader: Joseph Massey

Author Photo: Page Loudon

Table of Contents

Double-plush Wolf in a Hungry Age	9
don't you feel it's dangerous to want we're losing time *hurry hurry*	11
Dear Extinguished Individual	12
Eating the tender thing that will not fill	14
Goose Girl	15
gravicèmbalo col piano e forte	16
the body's steam rolling out	18
Romance #1 in G Major	21
The God Chain	22
The Greenest Body	23
We Lived in Mechanicsville	26
A bee in a yellow dress appears	27
ptomaine dance with Jumbo Bear	28
If I am speechless, would love be a mouth?	30
An Ode to Drunkenness and Other Criminal Activities	32
Arthur Murray's Dance Dictionary in Common Time	33
The cook had to salt them, and the wicked queen ate them	35
Thank You Dr. Grafenberg	36
Cadaver Dogs	37
Where are my small incidents, the blood poured from the shoes?	48
inside the smallest fury	49
Who Breathes Perfectly Under Water	51
What I didn't say when the gasworks shook their iron tails in my direction	52

L'Orchestre du Roi Soleil	53
Sock Monkey Directions	54
The Eternal Leer of the Playground Bully	55
The White Orchard	56
Groom	57
Laundress	59
like a raymond scott saint in my bed	61
Giving praise to sleek	62
spidergirl	64
the reptile monarchies	65
ragtown	67
Victorville Carnivàle	69
Pinwheel	71
I just thought it needed to be said	72
3 a.m. in the hemiola hospital	73
I will not sing the death of Dog	74
Credits	77
Acknowlegments	79

For Brown Dog, Poobah, Tom Dooley, Joe, Ginger, Teddy, Crazy Legs, Little Cat, Kelly, Bucket, Gideon, Baby, Ma, Smoky Joe, Fledge, Candy, Beethoven, Max Headroom, Pantages, Joey, Little out-of-the-wall, Simon, Shantie, Jeeves, Lloyd, Butch, Daphne, Zoe, Duncan, Buddy, Thelma, Megan, Winky, Klöie, Ophelia, Lars, Cruiser, Yogi, Bantu, Paris the Genius Cat and Orlando

Double-plush Wolf in a Hungry Age

A wax snout is a lot of work for a city
girl living in the forest, even counting
the enchantments.

I bought the wire at a shop
near 5 Mile Prairie. I am a seamstress.

> *My needles are signs*
> *My needles are sleeping children*

Go to hell. Some patterns are unspeakable.
But back to my story.
The dogs' plush undercoats
and broad heads have stopped breathing.

> *It would be easy*
> *To judge me as cruel*

I basted my pointy teeth.
They're white as *Betty Crocker Potato Buds*,
almost. My tongue is felt, the rusty
hole in the door of the medicine cabinet,
plumed tail my own.

A bit of fur glued on and some fork tines
and my transformation was complete. I was
the little man in the brown suit your mother
warned you about.

> *There is a simple cure:*
> *Lemon juice*
> *Breast milk*
> *Blood-letting*

I sew night and day. I carry my papier-mâché
ears straight up. I *nibble nibble nibble*
the center of your sweetbread heart.

don't you feel it's dangerous to want we're losing time *hurry hurry*

sweet and pungent your body having spilled
your shaved neck raw
the wasp crawls deeper into the fig
my tips swollen with it

today the bird census came to my house
to find the kingfisher's errant nest
I did not entice them though I feel criminal
like my second husband whose name I stole
he of the golden body hair quiet as a pet
I won't get over it   he left a welt

my house drowns
I crawl naked toward you on the floor
white and dark meat the dark
full of blood

I ask to be blindfolded
you smell like grass
and charred steak
with lemon pepper   on a gold charger
a new evangelism

paris the genius cat is in the yard stalking the bird
his heart clapping so fast
it's become   its own animal

Dear Extinguished Individual

      (it felt like an experiment at first)
a gold tooth simmered in the nest
clogged with hair
      (and later debased)

all your hoopla
an ovary-red dress
pointy shoes clacking down the stairs
molotov cocktail down the stairs
flat on my face as usual
rag wick showing

I sleepwalk now wake washing
my hands in the kitchen sink
green light

                (& eels under the floor)

my brain on zero skin gleaming
call it an *episode*
call it *appetite*

                MY VOICE GREW))))))))

a cartoon
in the undergarden
the dilatory moon seated firm

           and and and

I found a pearl button inside
its integument burned
I replaced the dogs' throats
with radios
my most lovely artifice

Eating the tender thing that will not fill

1.
There is a bruise on your jaw, a stone
or a broken tooth, teeth little Gullivers
in a row, a trip on a sidecar gone loose
from its mate and dropped
back into the quarry.

2.
There are odd punishments afoot.
For instance, the time you ate
your brother after cooking him
in a port reduction and *fatfatfat*
no take-backs.

4.
Mars hangs above you like a meat chime.

5.
At the last minute, twine knotted around your feet,
horse, raccoon, cat, dog, rabbit, lamb, pig, bear,
you can hardly sleep from all the racket in your bed
and spring, yes, the spring market is near.

Goose Girl

Snapped him wide open,
spine in her teeth,
three drops of blood, flutter,
a series of shocks.

She was late, too late for him,
an enchantment, his secret.

He forgot what it was like to stand
in the forest and bleed, pressed,
tied, silenced but for the false
dark with mink eyelashes.

There was the lesson of compliance.
There was the animal's head encased in plastic —
sooner or later the gas had to find a way.

There was no letting up once she started peeling
the skin off her heel, shed her entire, a little hissing
fit, don't call it, don't call it fit.

A criminologist found the truth
by stains on her dress, pink skin
underneath and the bees
gathered on her heel.

gravicèmbalo col piano e forte

last night a bear wandered through
shot by a rook
and more bears
dog circled   her welting box

I looked away

you bent me to the floor
my little grove on fire
the prairie slinging vibrant dresses

your uniform excited me as crisp things do
I wore your cap   aviator shirt
epaulets
zip tie   (stripes)   (wings)

bear crouched on the lawn
dog growled with all her gums
brillo bones in her kitchen
the smell of soap swoon

last night you said I kicked you 23 times
asleep
running running
in my eyelet sheets

a bear
loose in the garden
my teeth just right

boom boom boom

I was your pet
claws clacking down the stairs
I couldn't work the levers
I wanted to be human for you

the body's steam rolling out

I never hurt

        (my son never)
        but there inside
        there was hurt

I don't know how   he's not telling

river rocks explode in a camp fire
we thought it was funny
a known thing

I am an electric spine
I house the horse's skull
a flat distance from Spokane's
cold winter cold body frozencold
the river   the toll bridge

        good girls living under
        Hey Culligan Man!
        swinging ropes around our feet

      There's a world where I can go and tell my secrets to
        in my room   *in my room*

perfumed cream
a butterfly bush
flanked by cats
a sable brush
a small fur sex and gold   and gold

powder for my throat

§

we are a story problem
we are on a train headed east
the train travels X miles an hour
we share a berth and so
I straddle you like a German explorer
my wings my one good wing opening
and

(   )

I sing *Alive Alive O*

the power drill cries *Nooooo*
the power drill is not happy

              bevel *shoop shoop*
                router bit *shoop shoop*
cut and saw
wood gives voice
spring into it
anchor your wrist bone
your cabriole legs

what is the worth of a finger
a hand?

Romance #1 in G Major

I hate dreaming you, your face thick
enough to be sliced into luncheon meat.
Let me release the thin broth tadpole-
sticky lake from between my legs,
iridescent as slubbed silk.

We had a party with Wanda Jackson,
rummaged in her reptile pocketbook,
and after, witnessed a hit and run.
You called for help in your tiger suit,
chewed whiskers, *oh so fine*.

I sat on the floor cross-legged, turning
on and off the faucet of your desire.
The butcher taught me how
to wrap you in caul fat
and seal the seams.

The secret is to strain everything
through cheesecloth or chinoise.
This instruction is to *sear*.
This instruction is holy.

The God Chain
Priest River, Idaho

Anchor sheen trout tulip under yellow wood flicks its goose aside, holds hot the malediction kitchen march, oh marvelous me puddle pulsing the river's run. He speaks static, flicks the bristled coat and ducklings disappear easier into every field's floor. It is an arrow bath clogging and cracking the code under the milk skirt snow.

The Greenest Body

September full of crave
my alarming
glowy health like a genuine piece of the
                                            TRUE CROSS

I ate a nutria sandwich
entered the obvious portals   pear tree
                                        Glenn Gould's chair

watched a boy upside down in the bottom window of a school bus
talked about the dead woman
the movie star as if she never lived
I wanted to be her   I want want wanted

                                clôture

§

WE KNOW WHERE YOU'RE HEADED

everyone knew where I was headed all signs clear
reverberated with inflection gray bodies gliding the bridge
closed to traffic   noise   boats lit at night like factories

I failed the test I chose the wrong word
dogs in the bulkhead door turned their heads away
named   *Lux*
named   *Aurora*

I was their horizontal stabilizer
my body merely complex
equations of wave form
floated the pool in my red swimsuit
Hey Mary Mary count your fingers
you might be Harold Lloyd you might
explode accidentally

§

shoot your cuffs
shoot the moon
shoot a pullet   *shoot me*
[please]

§

fight your dogs big bets big money
shoot them when they lose
is this a crime
do it again in slow motion
now you're famous
shiver put your hands in your pants
sing *Zip-a-dee-doo-dah*

§

I swam in a warm hospital sheet
have you been   *have you*
in another country
when   I couldn't be sure

have you traveled to a foreign country
I was happy   I couldn't help it
love pushed my entire body lengthwise
through a mathematician's sieve
except for my steel-hitched ribcage
the damage was colossal

We Lived in Mechanicsville

You sniffed glue in your tube sock
I left kettles on the stove to burn
Was slow to give thanks for mice chewing
Through light fixtures splints on wrist
And knee how tired they became constant
Shivering teeth curving through the upper
Jaw sick with frost fog an excess of fat
In the heart hobbled together on your desk
Clear plastic skin red lines squiggled
Pulmonary coronary systemic 5 litres
You wanted a Brazilian woman in a bikini
How extraordinary the gluteus maximus
The external oblique in torn tunnels
Which you stroked breathing the wet hair
You imagined a more delicate version
An invisible woman who knew
When to staunch when to bleed

A bee in a yellow dress appears

When the change comes
it will be severe
it will be a drowning
it will be a plane crash
it will be the boy from honor camp who waved to me across
the lake when I was 12 followed me home stood outside my
window for 16 days whispering *I'm going to kill you*

he meant it that boy that boy

I am out of time
bind my ankles with a *Flo-Motion* jump rope
barter
suffocate
penny farthing bicycle
propped against the shed
I love these biting games
pinching games
slapping games
what will you trade
this time
what will you take
what will you
what

ptomaine dance with Jumbo Bear

there was no other way to do it debouch become invisible :: I left a key under the toad's frightful jaw was announced with zeal from the megaphone :: today's lesson :: never begin the conversation by saying *I'm hard* :: I know what a kiss means sing karaoke at the ossuary you've not eaten you'll be punished kiss me *hard* :: lurching attractant I wore a wool cap in the rain my hair increased the odds of filling your tag :: a password was given me by a man who died waiting for a limo I should never have left him I was forced to swallow oh little petri dish

Jumbo Bear inside *the bob*

free range 8 burners 2 ovens a variety of entry points :: you wanted his head both eyes X X *Wundertone* grease worked into fur :: *listen* the child king in the ground :: I rolled you like biscuits across Swan Front ear pressed to snow *listen god damn you* his slow heart under :: I was ashamed :: fire sprang from my heels hair threaded in the vireo's nest I tore your lottery tag :: where did you go to spot and stalk boil my bite hide a spoon a stiff-bristled brush a small knife :: how transcendent and loose I became later by the fire

A corn-fed beefswelling tempts Jumbo Bear

I wrote my name more than fifteen times which meant at least one person cropped up like fur in a plate of buttered beets :: I wanted to shave it nothing more than a device to get you into my mouth :: write *amen* at the end of your sentence please do not pronounce sentence *sennence* :: I patched the hole in my embouchure moist came through my warm machine :: at it again in the sink red carbolic *Lifebuoy* :: seriously if a woman is going to wash this often she should have her own scalpel

Jumbo Bear divines peril in a bucket of goat entrails

I welcomed the dryness your absence brought :: removed a Montana sized splinter from my squat bulk :: an owl flew past holding the limp body of a snowshoe hare :: your wife dangled polyps in her cup and I was on my belly again in the bed with the eyelet sheets :: there is dread in telling these stories little maps no control skin crashing against oozey clamor :: I wanted you to rise in the owl's talons I wanted to hurt you :: the animal *takes* the animal knows how to secure food :: *do you see now* :: I could not fit any more in :: there is an arm that curls there is a spine but there is no mouth :: this is what you forgot in your hurry :: there is no mouth

If I am speechless, would love be a mouth?
                    Jeanette Winterson, *Gut Symmetries*

bees inside the corn husk
blatant silk
royal jelly
night swung its sugary gardenia stick

        and so it rained
        for 97 days

we dined on the roof gerald and I
held the business end of a lightning rod
religious conversion
gerald's hands on the electric fence

        the body he said *is a great conductor*

a horse laid his head in my lap
I could hardly breathe the oh the oh the
christmas crisp rough fur
they were steam cleaning the streets
of vienna for Mozart's birthday

        a bee-cloud all around
        humming wet between
        baroque and revolution

we had a conversation about the girls
that died one from each school
murder suicide found in an apartment
a forest clearing a fishing shack
by the river

gerald spoke in tongues

there is a banquet inside me
candied and perfumed there is
lonely and there is
there is
good

Oh lamb of God, I come, I come

An Ode to Drunkenness and Other Criminal Activities

How much easier it would have been if you had simply
disappeared instead of becoming frozen inside the magnolia.
There is formaldehyde, there is a brisket for dinner.
You might be sated. You help yourself to your neighbor's
lilacs, iris, peonies, and later, the Sunday *New York Times*
shivering in its blue bag on their lawn.

These small acts, the cat whose back you snapped,
saw it flip and twist in your rearview mirror, it was dark,
it was raining, it was too late for you to stop or get help.
Sometimes it is a crime and sometimes it is a crime to love
your husband's brother. His story, the wine, the sad fumbling
of clothes. The trick is to remember everything.

There is a cupboard of broken-spined animals
and faithful amusements in the context of muscle,
of fat, and even in this soap opera the maid has bad
teeth and wants to sing. She serves you faithfully
but can never be as beautiful, an eye opening only
to itself. You are a nervous girl, plucking on your hem.
You put it in your mouth, you put everything
in your mouth.

Arthur Murray's Dance Dictionary in Common Time

Tom Hart drove his Chevy into the sea —
fat balloon slicks, suicide doors.
I pried him open from the middle,
past the farms, shovel-square lake,

wasp nest lanterns, cartoon
whirly-gigs, broken down
canoes, cows *lowlowlowing*,
seagull statues, anchors,

mailboxes, horses, burl
along the banks of the mudflat,
salmon smoke low in the huts,
salt fires, brine.

The locals share their beer
and *Cheetos*. They all want
to be Betty, want the bang,
the ecstasy, the conversion.

I waited for him to disappear
like bleach in the church parking lot,
the Mexican Canadian Elvis voting
for himself, stuffing the ballot box

in the *Cocktails/Card Room* lobby.
I invented a new way of drinking
tequila. I would have been his
Beulah Land.

I visit God's house
in a variety of disguises —
a wolf's head sewn to my head,
perfume, beetle-rich moss.

It's good to hide the smell
with smoke and incantations.
It even cures cancer.
Open the windows, Tom.

Gulls drop jellyfish into the yard.
I'm building a fire to reach you.
I'm burning away the night.
Don't forget your shoes.

The cook had to salt them, and the wicked queen ate them

She confused love of the body
with love of the mind, milk-fed,
wet all the time, prone to swagger.
Hey girly, the thick man said, *you are
so spangly with your cricket legs,
pink frizz everywhere*, and they slow
danced, her hand on his face
as always.

Hello? Hello? A bear on the phone,
black as the wood around her mirror.
She promised him salmonberries
and daffodils and long licks of heat
in the dead middle of winter. He
bought it.

She liked the tango. He bent her back
as the trumpet spit gasoline and groaned,
a *MovieTone* moment, one Queen or another
baking razor blades into a Christmas pudding,
descending in an ebony coat.

Thank You Dr. Grafenberg

maybe I gave up
touched the flooded head

in the morning everything is clear

when I look to the right
I see bodies flick inside the current
they are   radiant antennae

maybe I am a criminal after all
an enchantment a talking dog
save me

Cadaver Dogs

§

the electricity meter spins and spins
you yell *what makes it spin like that
what source of power are you abusing*
I was not awake and something heavy
with a tail crawled across the roof
every night against rough pips and edges
you were bruised and you lied
we'll talk again when your children
have sewn razor blades to their lips
the displacements that powered them
into your world stop yourself now
stop and build a prayer card
a double great novena to god
dilating in the clinic reborn

§

§

held your wolf head up in stupid agreement
I forgot to cut the phone dog crouched
on the lawn ate all the fat aroused hiss
padpadpad ran toward us *little whore*
little biscuit paw greasy mouth urine hymn
tell me again what you said just before I felt it
coming hard knee buckle bright luciferin
breathed the machine of Ellensburg blue
beneath the Piper's bird body skimming wheat
fields car dealerships shook the sky out of my
pillow all the beaky meats in attendance
this was given this was taken I seeded the moon
you licked yourself like a human
laughed and kept laughing

§

§

astride the agile dog
lap-red tongue of Christ
quivernose
the smell the smell
night cracking open brother
carrying brother
in slippery teeth
be still be still now
desire me
there are miracles
wormy flank
shiverbright coat
sing into my mouth
O Obedient Animal

§

§

he asked *have you made specific plans*
for your suicide
I could drown on Chartres or Roanoke
grow fat astonished
my stomach rolled like yeasty dough
four paws around the earth beet stink
red dog mouth red throat-perfumed
with meat and three children waiting
for their mother down the street
under the porch the fleshy rim
tangled fur everywhere
I wash plates over and over
I am careful I make prayers
to the secret horticulture of animals

§

§

in summer need is greater
smells greater a greater
throb hums in my head
he says run *run*
sharp hurt tender paw mud nettles
in the hungry tree shoes a shirt
yip yip believe what lives
in the bottom of the lake
his voice beyond the canoe
beyond the dock swim muscle
darling scent yes it is my great
I find it I always find
cadaver dog the human leash
food at last your hands in my fur

§

§

you look everywhere for him sacrifice
one drunk husband for another
wait for the phone to wait it's so 1963
go-go boots pink hair tape it down
make it flat he'll love you more if
it's a perfect split curl *Dippity Do*
transistor radio flesh ear piece
the plastic leash to be beautiful
you sling a slab of frozen
meat on the counter he teaches
the boy to kill a rabid dog
you are full of bony excess
you think if you are beautiful
enough he will stay

§

§

gliding back and forth inside her
goodbye I said *goodbye*
goodbye goodbye goodbye
no one believed me damp between
gliding back and forth sleek and soft
I surfed the entire coast
bufflehead towns rutting my skin
his length his *ahh* inside me
damp night sloppy stinking tide
no one swam there
I let tomatoes split on the vine
hid under the rabbit hutch
stroked and sucked the quick
yeasty soil

§

§

tender I leaked from my side
raspy in dreamland
the lapdog slithered
from its nasty chain passed low
over Goldbar wing tipped
on the outside where knives
quick and sharp and quick
I didn't stand a chance
there was hard splendor in the hotel
a shape without air
convulsions directed the clouds
how tall was the ladder you shook
to find me how long
the milky strand

§

§

a blind peach poodle bumped into furniture
jumped on the boy's lap licking licking licking
the woman asked *isn't my little girl pretty*
isn't she shampooed and perfumed and pretty
just for Mama just for Mama just for Mama
then the parrot (there was a parrot too) started talking
I love you Mama I love you Mama I love you Mama
the boy saw her refrigerator covered with photographs
of peoples' children some cut
out of magazines later the boy asked me
did she molest other children
I didn't have an answer
I never considered it
I thought I was the only one

§

§

dog was used in the seduction
I staunched the wound with paper
later dog dragged the mess
from the trash chewed the wet corners
mother was ashamed father was ashamed
they all agreed *dog must love the family*
my right hand was cut
amputated in fact with antibiotics
gauze sterile instruments
morphine drip all on the up-and-up
in a religious ceremony dog sutured
the sore circumference ran with red
thread in his mouth drew in
pulled hard around the danger

§

§

night nurse starched cap bright
red cross blue stripe
needle sliding in and through
stitches straight as the edge
of a nun's handkerchief
imagine her private life
as a fairytale princess
trapped in a hospital or Harriet
Nelson her desperate hands
wiping and wiping the sterile
skin sluicing blood
from a puncture until it runs pink
lips puckered whispering
wound wound wound

§

Where are my small incidents, the blood poured from the shoes?
The Unabridged Journals of Sylvia Plath
Friday 13, 1959

A man on the freeway onramp
sits in an ornate chair. I wait
for the signal and he pushes
his snout into my car window.
He tells me *the horse dies*
at the end of the movie because
it's a Disney movie and in Disney
movies the animals
always die.

This is not news to me.
I've been trampled.
My foot was crushed.
I disappeared a twin —
ate her with tissue and salt,
my fingerprints on the stirrup.
She told me *never stop competing.*
Apologize for the blood in your mouth.
Change your oil.

Oh *Jiminy Cricket* in your stupid spats,
you are not the warm moist air
in the stall or hay or saddle or spur.
You are simply the horse that dies
at the end of the movie, the boy's
conscience, the ring of tiny sores
around the world's red mouth.

inside the smallest fury

for Zina Linnik

last night a raccoon scumbled through
my kitchen window the   *WE*   in her head
stinging drain cupboard the musty fruit room
pectin glossing her fur

CAUGHT CAUGHT CAUGHT

her throat knew as my throat knows
a steady tipping forward

I did nothing to save her

there is talk of a portal

*what would you take
if you were never coming back*

sneakstorm prosecco drive-thru cigarettes cherry juice /cherry
light my louche dress

in the city men in khakis and pinch shoes
feast on dungeness crab
frozen in doomspouts frozen
in diapers mascara glue limp handshakes
belching and farting pump quarters into the ridey
horse in front of Safeway as babies yelp

a red-tailed hawk marked his hunting boundary smelled
Bakelite smelled hackberry smelled my beautybow
I was in trouble I chose to contain it
accordion ribs black white ribs lunette lip
I forgot the dangers of a soft-bottomed river

the lights went on in Electric Park all the children
in a row that warm blinko day waving flags
a deep infatuation with sudden violent atmospheres
babbitt bearings sheared at the base

I am sorry you are not moving on

Who Breathes Perfectly Under Water

Bee stings my chest, split open,
a crappy diorama in *The Museum
of Civil War Medicine*. I was inside
forever, a wasp fucking a fig, flat,
laced in my own syrup, lungs
square felts pressed with steam.
A strange girl opened a wound
under my ribs, crawled in.
She makes me hungry, hungry
as an open suitcase, hungry
as Crater Lake. I feed her honey
and ripe little needles.

What I didn't say when the gasworks shook their iron tails in my direction

There is a foot-shaped stain on the end of my mattress like Sibelius snapping a white tablecloth across the Baltic Sea inviting me to tea. Night Dog thumps his body against my door. I've cut my hair to fiery nubs my angel hair my blonde angel cluttersuit. I eat a bowl of marrow beans and pound my feet but too many hours in the swamp prying goathead burrs out of my heel awakened more than triage more than language my caliche nerve. I don't know how to do it. I stand on my hind legs and bark. I want more. I want more. I want more.

L'Orchestre du Roi Soleil

the vein in your throat candle blackbody
heated to 1800 degrees K signals
the kingfisher's fat wobble dive down
you would be inside and alone if not for the
reflection of a rotted pear in a blue bucket
if not for sound ramming into your brain a huff
a steady beat a secret from mozart's dead mouth
you cannot even after all these years become
the girl you once risked o father o mother
clinical and acute you chew your fingers
on your knees in the sick garden tomatoes
green the grass slick and matted nothing
but an abnormality the frontal regions
bilateral in the feng caretaker's house
each terrifying breath the workstation's
glow the hissing fountain the small lake
small lake small lake small lacunar lake

Sock Monkey Directions
A found poem

Draw a line for your monkey's tail
Sew your monkey's arms
Sew your monkey's tail
Turn legs inside out

Cut your monkey's arms
Cut your monkey's tail

Secure your monkey's crotch
Stuff your monkey's crotch
Sew up your monkey's crotch
Trim your monkey's crotch

Attach your monkey's arms
Backstitch your monkey's mouth
Secure the ears with invisible stitching

The Eternal Leer of the Playground Bully

A clumsy ritual
you hang yourself
with your own striped tie.

You gnaw on leg of deer, rabbit, wild duck,
roasted turbot, grilled salmon. Hungry
for blood, you rub the stewed fruits
into your skin, fall asleep with the light on,
thumbsucker, biter.

Your father made you hunt.
You wanted to take me,
you were strong enough,
you had the goods.

Say it in 5 languages. Oberon
spools out of the kingfisher's mouth,
the mermaid's chorus. By the time
you noticed it was swollen,
ready to burst, a polyp
with double roots.

It was a prank.
It didn't mean a thing.
Sometimes people just die
accidentally.

The White Orchard

You said *sheath*, a short story,
a boy frozen in a lake. You said *builds
a fire, takes off her clothes, reads to him.*
It was simply a misunderstanding.
You meant *protein, effervescent.*

I poked holes in the ice with a blade
of grass, carried an axe, an empty pickle
jar. His eyes were open. His mouth formed
the word *prune*. He might have been
whistling. He wore corrective shoes.

You said *sheath*, I heard *tissue, flesh
envelope, champagne cocktail dress.*
There was a war room, and trout bent
in pale green reeds, a kind of sickness
like sleeping pills or barnacles.

You said *sheath*, and I heard *a tubular fold
of skin, a condom, a dog's penis retreating.*
I covered him with linen napkins.
My mistake.

Groom

a compulsion at best
the threat of bleach or other
corrosives
named her dogs (not truly hers)

Dog Regret
Dog Whimsy
and
Piece Dog the Lesser

snipped off their flops
with a sharp-tailed   **Q**
glued the membranes
to her pulse points
which had begun to decay
from age and Evil Deeds

there were grooves
around her upper legs
cotton and elastic pincers
hissed while smiling
bit sleeping children
shed mightily in porcelain
she had many names (truly hers)

Mrs Flinch
Mrs Preen
Mrs Can't-Leave-The-House-Without-My-Face

The Book of Animal Law
was lost to her The Book of Feral
The Book of Tender
with her new fur and pink skin
she was an exact
and well deserved appetite

Laundress

§

toadstools grew underneath
the galvanized bucket
round spongy knobs
she could lose an arm
in the wringer had seen it once
snap *snap*   snapping the sheets
the ginger hair'd girl stopped
at the shoulder

§

a brief symposium on bleach

      1. to make whiter
      2. to remove the color from
      3. degenerative and healing properties

§

her broken skin the spready
rash on her thighs bag balm lard lamp oil
rubbed into her hands
heels calves knees and grim

§

once she wore a green dress gathered tight
at the waist   *taffeta*
a word with its own steamsong
black stockings a chocolate garter
one foot on the train platform
a basket of pears a trip to rosary
head beach

§

the toadstools
sprouted fast overnight
like imps the nappies
of bad children she pushed
the sheets down with her stick
stirred the brown suds

§

injected herself with sugar
and starch
skirts hiked she felt
something brush against her legs
the rumor is she gave birth
to rabbits two pink and squalling
one died as soon as it sucked
breath the other lives in a cage
behind the tannery

like a raymond scott saint in my bed

a building floats down the street
a spaceship   lit   from the bottom
even in my sex I run flat out feet slamming
limbs   a storm tree
full of water

my drama played in houses
the rabbit house   the motorcycle house
the buffalo house   jitterbugging as branches
whip   the chicken coop

you are a prairie   a sibylline cornfield
asleep in the bastille tunnel

hurt me

it's easy
you remember how   your silky mouth
circular breathing
force your whole hand into radiant

Giving praise to sleek

1.

my skin a cat in a green bag out to sea
there was no love in me
even inside he thought of a new species
a wrecked oven
side by side
the twins cantered through the forest
one thick torso connecting them
hair plaited into a rooty braid
I wore a potato colored coat
stuck with thrashthorn bramble mud marram
each night I said *never again* I said
Stop and I meant it

2.

the train rocked us to Britenbush
I stood naked in the hot springs
because that is what he wanted
we volleyed through mountains
in the dark a man's hand circled my leg
he whispered *your ankles are small*
are you a grown girl?
I read *Bleak House* using a lark
as a bookmark its flattened spine

3.

while pregnant I shaved in hopes
of one deep cut my arm hair
not like the Vietnamese girls
who rubbed me who said *so round*
there was always work to be done in the bakery
an apron to wash mouse turds on the floor
women twittered in the break room
bells the sharp mixing blades
time clock my hair sprung with flour
stiff with dough we played statues
who will drop the long pan tonight
who will pinch her finger in a gear

4.

I remember the exact moment
I unhooked my dress
everyone watched me step
into the Wenatchee River
wade across slimy rocks
talk shop with Jesus
they applauded and later
fed me cake and organic rice
he followed me to the bathroom
where I fell into the slipper tub and sank
my hair a milfoil sheen on top

spidergirl

into the cackleberry
ripe with snowbees
a noise pounded
my night window open
cougar the white chicken
in its mouth cracked the spine
such a noise oh god
oh god shook me *I didn't look*
listened from a great distance
my spine bent reciprocated
in the excellent ritzville wheat
burst forth with radiance

the reptile monarchies

i
your wives in a row cows in a row leak
milk into iron buckets have grown sleek
have scalded our nipples
have electric hair

ii
fuchsia inside the salmon's mouth dogs joyous in the creek dogs ate
chum joyous in the creek broke the trittica moon

iii
water behaving as fire
froze to death in a railroad station
DO NOT CALL   DO NOT CALL ME
DO NOT CALL Christ with the pleading already
it's an earwig wedding

iv
Tom Blue Tom Blue blue Nova
let's get raw *tomtom tomcat tomblue*
drunk all the time black and blue blond and blue
shhh now I told you
hush

v
one more minute in that house with the goat
the empty upstairs room the window-seat
you shot speed drew naked girls at night
with a ballpoint pen
I was not the pouch you needed
had it out with your brother I did I did
do you still want to know how it was
animalcule

vi
all that's up top is mindless root-hog clutter

vii
what mysterious assemblage was created I fled polished beveled I was not like your other wives keening nickering this meant nothing David/Goliath swinging your sling simply a mid-flight chase a brief place between toxic and beauty I carved it with my knife felt it in the rocks the creek my hair drifted on the fire's current my strong arms dug postholes in that country I heard my blood scribed from my body's stars Canis Major Canis Minor Lupus Sirius at night a mercury vapor lamp pushed back the cedar thickets

viii
when I was a girl
I worked in a factory
sewed fox tails to the collars
of womens' coats
I was fast my fingers pinched fur to wool
heavy motors whirred below
I was paid well with company picnics
overtime corn chowder feeds
we sang at our machines
we sang pulling fur from our throats

ragtown

    fingered her baubles   the ruby deluge &
    brought the rubber
    tulips up with her
    mouth

100
101
102
103 degrees

switchblade eyeballs
goblins bit her hip
attended by doctors
her house swallowed
tuss & flapping miles of film

no   wait

their love was an ocelot in a flamingo's beak

(fever is a cheap drunk)

she named him
she named him
she named him
all the way through

carburetor junkie
slick cool mud
tactus

Victorville Carnivàle

I was pocket sized
with a teensy weensy voice
my clothes never dry
the weight of a wool coat
I gave up dancing
the smug blue toaster
goddamn the men
pounding my roof
with mallets

one night my one night alone with the beast fork-ed tongue bitten down nails I baked cookies for children attended by the fragrant bodies of animals cats the giant gold dog the baby with its steel arm and hook sewn to a cloth bunny swung from the door frame

if I were a dead fish
in a creek and a dog
picked me up
with his slick teeth
and rolled me
and rolled *in* me
and rolled me into
his honest fur
would this be
true love?

I lied to the men on the roof told them I had a piano lesson to teach *pack it up now* I said in my grouty voice I told them the false student was about to arrive I said *no no you cannot use* my bathroom christ what was up with those men mend the shingles fix the roof liars down on all fours

Pinwheel

I was tending the garden when a bee flew
up my blouse stung my left nipple
I was claimed then
I wanted to be a better woman
reaching back with a corked finger
into fruit
I carry ice
worship fur

My body is split
& wet in spite of alcohol
with the goaty head man
nails curling down
becoming cloven
I'm not alarmed
I like the pillow
slick

I fold the clothes of my dead
into plastic bags dresses shirts
socks slippers the whole shebang
my dead smell like lemons
their teeth are marshmallow white
my sister is perfect
she has a perfect body
her hair is a gold wasp's nest
I fold her *Snow White* pajamas
into a square

I see the reptile man on television
& realize it is my husband
holding a two-headed turtle to the camera
all three of them smile

I just thought it needed to be said

Don't take it seriously
I got caught peeking behind the curtain
I slapped you hard on the cheek like Balzac's eyehole
I retained grace
I was a small animal trainer
I put medicine on my cat and he hid from me
I found him in my cupboard glaring
How did he pull the cupboard door closed behind himself
Next week my brain lies in transaxial slices
A beam of x-ray shot right through my head
Attenuation Blunting Algorithms
I should have paid attention
Left is shown at right
This has nothing to do with the bees in my hair or the burning

3 a.m. in the hemiola hospital

convinced the entire frog world
was inside she knelt and dug

lit from underneath by flood lamps   shapeless
in her night gown her treaties

the garden held its breath in her kitchen
topsoil on the floor she   fragrant from his body

a taxi waited between the pepper trees

wore a greatcoat
pockets stuffed with seeds & a star-nosed mole

mud puckered paws
concubine buckles

her coat gathered leaves and twigs
moss beetles toadstools until

she became the forest a root
transformed

now that the yeast had proofed for 17 years
& nothing warned of poison

they walked through the fritillaries
children drove miniature cars along the seawall

blue orchard bees drenched in pollen
landed on every surface of her house

pried her mouth open   a prayer
consequence

I will not sing the death of Dog
Maxine Kumin

imagine the worst thing that could happen
dog runs upstairs owl tufts in his mouth
thumps his tail drums an entire processional
so great is his sorrow

imagine the worst thing that could happen
to a woman like you a bitch a chine spread
open on the hearth drying as hornflies
do their work on your shoulders your back

imagine the worst thing that could happen
in the bide-a-wee the lick ballroom sick
with yellow tulips the promise of yellow
chew toys strewn on the carpet

imagine the worst thing that could happen
eyelid scald seizure rooty mole
a blood excavation lump
growing inside your brain

Now.

drive fast at night on a rainy street
drive fast with your lights off seatbelt slack
drive so fast sound disappears
roll down your window and scream

Then.

grow out of your own chalk line
your elephantine desire your gummy insides
the owls sit one by one on your outstretched arm
tame familiar with your scent

Credits

"If I am speechless, would love be a mouth?"
Gut Symmetries
Jeanette Winterson
Alfred A. Knopf, 1998
ISBN: 978-0-676-97102-6 (0-676-97102-4)

"Where are my small incidents, the blood poured from the shoes?"
The Unabridged Journals of Sylvia Plath
Sylvia Plath, Karen V. Kukil (Editor)
Anchor Books, 2000
ISBN-13: 9780385720250
ISBN: 0385720254

"I will not sing the death of Dog"
from "One Small Death in May"
Our Ground Time Here Will Be Brief
New and Selected Poems by Maxine Kumin
Penguin Books, 1982
ISBN -13: 9780140422986
ISBN: 0140422986

Acknowlegments

Thank you to the following journals in which some of these poems have appeared.

Anti-, Barn Owl Review, Burnside Review, Caffeine Destiny, Columbia Poetry Review, Cranky, Death Metal Poetry, Diode, Elixir, Lungfull!, Many Mountains Moving, No Tell Motel, Pistola, Sawbuck, The Bedside Guide to No Tell Motel – Second Floor, The Concher and Verse Daily.

Thank you to Page Loudon for his patience, art and love. Thank you to Reb Livingston, editor extraordinaire, for her brilliance and friendship. Thank you to Kelly Bokyer, Susan Butler, Beth Coyote, Laura Gamache, Pat Hurshell, Nancy Ibsen, Marta Sanchez and Martha Vallely for filling my house with poetry and warmth while I was working on these poems.

About the Author

Photo Credit: Page Loudon

Rebecca Loudon lives and writes in Seattle, Washington. She is the author of *Tarantella* and *Radish King* (Ravenna Press) and *Navigate, Amelia Earhart's Letters Home* (No Tell Books). She is a violinist and teaches violin lessons to children.

Also by No Tell Books

2008

PERSONATIONSKIN, by Karl Parker

2007

The Bedside Guide to No Tell Motel – 2nd Floor, editors Reb Livingston & Molly Arden

Harlot, by Jill Alexander Essbaum

Never Cry Woof, by Shafer Hall

Shy Green Fields, by Hugh Behm-Steinberg

The Myth of the Simple Machines, by Laurel Snyder

2006

The Bedside Guide to No Tell Motel, editors Reb Livingston & Molly Arden

Elapsing Speedway Organism, by Bruce Covey

The Attention Lesson, by PF Potvin

Navigate, Amelia Earhart's Letters Home, by Rebecca Loudon

Wanton Textiles, by Reb Livingston & Ravi Shankar

notellbooks.org

www.ingramcontent.com/pod-product-compliance
Lightning Source LLC
Chambersburg PA
CBHW031209090426
42736CB00009B/843